Cascading Emotions

G Jayashankar Menon

INDIA • SINGAPORE • MALAYSIA

ISBN 979-8-89277-802-2

Contents

Cascading Emotions

Emotions cascade through
These knowing eyes
It is as though all I know
Has been clouded
By the avalanche
Of Icy feelings and
Heartfelt remorse
These eyes have felt
The burning embers
Of anger and despondency
By repeated failures
And abject poverty
In the dull days of extreme sadness
Everyone would reject me
With no sense of sympathy
Or compassion
I guess the lessons learnt are Umpteen
To last one's lifetime!

Drops of Joy

The Happiness I have known
Has been very rare indeed
Between milestones of remorse
I wish this lasts
A lifetime
Or is it too good to last
Is it your guess or Mine
I need to go on
With a sense of patient alacrity
Lest all that I had done
Becomes Undone
It is a threat
That is always there
Round the corner
Now that Freedom is here
I guess better times are there Up Ahead!!

Maddening Darkness

There are so many things
Occurring, no meaning
Or Method in the repetition
The faith required
To withstand the onslaught
Has taken gigantic strength
Perhaps, the results too
Have been colossal
My ways, Direct Road ahead
Because looking at the mirrors
Have yielded no result
Except other than,
Avoiding the spells and
Thorny pricks of
The ways and byways,
Taken in the days
Of the mysterious unexplained
Unfathomable darkness.
There must have been
A method in the sheer madness
For the outcome
Thereafter, the fighting back
With valour
Barring no Hold!!
As the scriptures Beckoned!!

The Holy War

The world is a myriad
Layer of confusion
No thought directed at solving
The gigantic problems
Or imbalances
Can set things right
Or bring about a proper way
I was taught
To be polite and decent
But when things became wild
And the onslaught was relentless
I had no other way
But to fight back
As Arjuna the kshatriya warrior
Was taught and beckoned
To fight an epic holy war!
By the Lord Himself

Peaceful Lotuses

I thought I was mesmerised
By the continuous pain
On a mental Plain
But now I believe
It was all,
That just passed.
I truly had to put
In an effort
That only the Almighty
Could support and encourage
It is not just in passing
The real experience
Of a soul tormented
Continually and viciously burnt
As though there was
No end in sight,
Only a corpse standing in vain,
Now I see yonder
A blue lake, with still waters
With a dozen of pink red lotuses
The peace that is, is an experience
Not had for ages together!!

Of Duty and Valour

The world is spinning around
It is the blazing sun
Shining high up above
We were mortals
Struggling with our egos
To make it big
Even though we have realised
We are just specks of dust
In the desert sand.
Of what use all this, we might think
But God our saviour,
Has beseeched us to fight on
Till we reach our pristine Glory
For Honor it is, that only matters
In this reverberating pulsating Life
We need a guiding star
To help us through
The travails of riding
Out the stormy seas.
A battle it is, waged
Bloodshed does not matter
For we shall keep our Heads
Held high, whatever challenges
That come our way.

For Mother Earth
Keeps doing Her job,
Spinning 'round and spinning around!!

Of Heaven and Hell!

There is nothing in the World
That can tear me down
I have reached so high
I want to be climbing higher
There is no place left
That God has marked untouched
I want to reach
The Highest High
'Coz, I know
I have been at the low of the lowest ebbs
Nothing can stop me now
Having faced the brutality
Of the Truth that
Has just passed by
My descendants will be carrying
The legacy I have left behind
So now, I realise it is very harsh,
There is little Time left
For me to prove a Point
Before the Sword has found
Its place again on the Mantle
Apparently, it's keen sharpness
Is asking for some more Bloodshed
Before some soldiers and pawns

Have been cast asunder
Running Helter Skelter
For refuge in a place
Actually, meant only for Prisoners
Who have nothing but Hell to choose.

The Forced Road

I have suffered enough
Why is it that I still am
Even though the chains
Have been unshackled
Feels like those chains
Are still around me
Gotten used to it
Life has been one long Pain
The people who have played
Have been just excuses
For my pain Points
Never been able to address, though!!
I am still at the starting point
Some people calling themselves Fathers
Have played their roles
Worse than Grand children
Such has been my experience
God Forbid, no one else
Goes through the road, I have been forced through!!

Lady Car Drivers

They are all over the place
Large goggles to prove
None can match
Their performance on the Road
They block the roads
All the men wait
In perplexed askance
As to their turn for the green light
It is now their Fad
To take the steering wheel
And possess all the traffic snarls
As though none would
Disobey their orders
They come in all hues and sizes
Femineity at their core
False influenced ideologies
By friends and families galore!

An Epic Called Life

Truth becomes null
Difficult to digest
When those closest are
Unable to understand
The voices bellowing
In my Heart
I have to chant
Outwardly for allowing
To listen to pain
Going on within
Till all those
Who but have to listen
Just turn away
Wanting avoidance
Of the glaring Truth
My sacrifice
Has been unfathomable
As my plight
Is taken for granted
By those around
The Pain is wicked
Feels like I had gone a wrong path
Too hasty to choose
And had life changing

Ramifications, until now
Guess this holiday
Is fitting, to find my roots
And make things happen again
For the world to enjoy!!

A Friend Beckons

It is like an illusion
Never thought it so bad
The world is going round and round
It is the same static as it ever was

I prefer to be on the sides
Rather than in the mainstream
The winds have chipped
My boat and left me asunder

I feel like I need a solace
To keep my heart going
There is nothing less
Than confused times causing more remorse.

My old friend keeps calling me
To remind me of happy times of the Past
I wish he solved my present gruel
To keep me sailing on happy ever after!

The Frothy Beaches

The seas melt into the Horizon
Until the skies and the ocean become One
My world belongs to the Green Forests
Forming a line by the sea coasts

The crabs jump out of the sands
Crawling towards the rugged shores
While the fishermen cast their boats on the beach,
After they have returned, with their fish filled nets

I look on from the shack
At the edge of the green foliage
Seeing if anything was amiss
From the picture-perfect scenery

Watch the seagulls whisking away a fish or two
From the fisherman's catch
Not wanting to poke their sharp beaks
Into the frothy and salty seawaters

The Merciful One

Of God and His ways
I bow down to Him
Forever as He beckons
Me onward, towards activity and Solace

His ways are most cherished
Although treading towards His path
Is the most wearisome and tiresome
But the road ahead is worth the challenge

I believe in His Magnanimity
And His endless Mercy
For He has forgiven me even
My most Heinous mistakes and crimes

Oh God Almighty
I kneel down to you
For your Blessed mercy
Keeps me away from foes and stressful troubles!!

The Green Grease

Money is what everyone wants
This life on our Lonely Planet
Happens when the Green Bucks
Move Hands or stays in bank lockers

My world was centred
Around it for ages
Forgotten in the Labyrinth
Of several failed attempts and a few passes

Has anyone taught
Me the value
Of true success
Which need not translate to money

Many big billionaires
Have made it on sheer luck
I wondered if I too
Could make it on the Big List!

Mystery Tunnel

What I see yonder
Is but huge boulders
And pits on the way
Treacherous serpents coiling at every turn

Wondered always, as I breathe hard
Why I am placed
At such a focal point
When everyone else took it so easy

My world is stuffed with mundane work
There is no light
Except for the glare
Of the burning embers deep in my heart

Suddenly it all seems so right
As I jot down, a mystery to me,
What I always wanted has arrived
The tunnel just opened up to the blue skies Yonder!

Paradise Calling

The malls look overcrowded
I ask myself
Where do these people come from
The escalators and lifts working nonstop

The shops therein look empty
Seems weird
The food-courts
Always full

Is eating here just a fancy
To fulfil one's appetite
For the extraordinary
An escape from the mundane and dreary existence

The shimmering lights
The ever-sprouting fountains
Beacon a Paradise
A world all its own

Until one comes out with numbing ecstasy
From the feature film or
The airconditioned shopping alleys
Only to return a week or two later!

Dreaded to Loved

He comes in many forms
Never can anticipate
When he ventures
Into our ordinary lives

A disaster here and
A failure there
Many losses encountered
Even without our consciousness

I look on helplessly
And wait for the Tide
To ride out
For the 71/2 years to pass

Saturn makes us stronger
More intelligent and smart
But all the more Humble
In every step at the end of it all

He has punished me
For all my bad karmas
Cannot escape his clutches
For punishment is certain as are his rewards!

His blue form
I bow down to, most venerable one
As I now embrace Him
For He is my very own Friend!

Grace Be to God

Oh Lord Saibaba
You beckon me
Towards you
Your eyes radiate, attracting all!

I love your form
As I surrender to you
You have cast a spell on me
A miracle you had devised, for me, unknown

You have emancipated me
From all the troubles
That seemingly never got over
As today I walk with you

I fear no one
As your grace is manifold
Please forgive me for my sins
You are for ever my Guiding Light!

The Eternal Spark

People seem to mock at me
For my stance as I approach them
Makes me uncomfortable
Cannot help but resist the helplessness

What more do I need to do
Whilst all trials and tribulations
Seem to have passed
Is there anymore round the corner I wonder

The bucks don't seem to be coming
Working hard and knocking
At all given doors
The listless feeling is now a habit

Can anyone shower me with compassion
For many failures and losses, this wanderlust has faced
Hope is the only spark in my heart
To keep me going through this dry spell!

The World – A Quagmire It Is

Things happen in this
Dynamic Space and Time
Wont of any control
Without any Rhyme or Reason

It is but apparent confusion
Not to be foretold
Almost as though
It is but destined to happen

Nothing is there
In these bare helpless hands
All are but silent onlookers
Of Glory and Defeat both just passing by

People give vent
To pent emotions with varied strength
All Epics have described various battles
This Quagmire too, would find its way among the stories of Time

Soulful Music

The music floats through the cool air
It cringes at my heart
Some emotion trapped inside
Waiting for it to erupt, at the slightest pretext

Things wait on the bridge
As the melodies pass through
My world is not the same
Ever after having listened to this song, a million times

I don't want to rest
Till I get a solution
For the cries in this music make one believe
That my ears would address to the singer's agony

The tears almost smack these dry lips
And wait for the boat to arrive
On the river banks, below the bridge
Where I walked to, eager to find solace in the song as it was eager to end!

Unexplained Sadness

She went past him
As though he never meant anything
The pretence she bespoke
Left him bewildered as he saw her pass.

He felt like calling out as he stumbled
But his throat felt dry and hoarse
The moment just passed
He lifted his hand beckoning her, but to no avail.

It felt like she was running
At a pace faster than before
Tired of being with him anymore
Probably she got wind, and looked for something better.

The brocade saree she wore
Shimmered in the night sky
Twinkling against his black seeing eyes
As she melted into the pale darkness until out of sight

Glorious Festivities

The music blares out loud
From the open grounds below
Ready to host the colourful dancers
The dandiyas clasped in every hand

The girls of every attire and age
Dance to the rhythm
The lights shine on them in the night
Adding to the mirth and joy of festivities

The Goddess looks on from the stage
In the distance, for it is Dussehra
Casting her divine look with her huge eyes
Upon the simple folk, spreading cheer.

The world now seems like
It has rid itself of all darkness and evil
Where everyone joins in the magic of the moment,
Bringing in new spells and vibrations, of the colourful days to come!

Goddess for Protection

Lo the eyes of mighty Kali
Ever Benevolent
Upon Her ardent Devotees
She casts Her magic spell upon all!

Justice, she delivers
Not hesitant to slay with her Cosmic Dance
On everything evil in her way
Drinks their blood, licked with Her red long tongue

Her thick hair falls upon Her shoulders
Like mane, black and straight
Her form ever so beauteous
Causes fear in the hearts, Her mighty hands a sight to behold!

Oh Goddess, ever so radiant
I bow down to you
In complete surrender
Seeking eternal deliverance, from all, small and sundry!

Bike Travel

It was a ride for serendipity
I loved the way the vehicle handled.
Only exception was the unwashed and unkempt tank
For long joy rides it's a good option, indeed.

It took a while to feel the horse
The power in between, it took me to through the roads.
Comfortable and velvety smooth,
Upon the black mettle zipping beneath the rubber tires

It is a rotation through the winds
Spokes brushing past holding on tight,
Into the rubber
The world captured in the moment, of the travelling Second.

The Ways of the Sun

The sun is what it is today
Red, casting hues all across the horizon
It was not the same yesterday, I am sure
Probably the clouds made the difference
And the position too
Every coming day is different in its flavor
The people who get up, doing
Their daily milieu.
The moods and thoughts keep changing
There is no escape.
The possibilities and events
Keep changing every passing moment
It is amazing how this world
Sustains itself
Amidst myriad differences and diversity.
The sun is always witness to all!

Flowers on a Wanton Day

The flowers upon the small little shrub
Put me in a tizzy.
It felt like a healing moment,
As I gazed at the colors from nowhere
It looked like they were headed somewhere
Riding on the dreams of a man who dwelt in nostalgia.

The flowerbed is what I thought
I would want in permanence in this screen,
That displayed the murals of life
Breathing deep into the pangs so real and
Seemingly endless suffering endured
Through the duties of the wanton day.

www.ingramcontent.com/pod-product-compliance
Lightning Source LLC
LaVergne TN
LVHW091237150826
845673LV00003B/1182